PRAYERS
FOR MY
17TH CHROMOSOME

AMIR RABIYAH

SIBLING RIVALRY PRESS
LITTLE ROCK, ARKANSAS
DISTURB / ENRAPTURE

Prayers for My 17th Chromosome
Copyright © 2017 by Amir Rabiyah
Cover art, *Centerpiece II*, by Manzel Bowman (www.manzel.biz)
Author photograph by Jadon Griffith
Cover design by Seth Pennington

Sibling Rivalry Press, LLC
PO Box 26147
Little Rock, AR 72221

info@siblingrivalrypress.com

www.siblingrivalrypress.com

ISBN: 978-1-943977-42-0

Library of Congress Control Number: 2017944196

This title is housed permanently in the Rare Books and Special Collections Vault of the Library of Congress.

First Sibling Rivalry Press Edition, November 2017
Second Sibling Rivalry Press Edition, June 2018

PRAYERS

FOR MY

17TH CHROMOSOME

IN LOVING MEMORY
OF DR. IBRAHIM FARAJAJÉ

CONTENTS

"HE'LL KNOW HOW TO FLOAT BETWEEN
TWO WORLDS SOMEDAY."

-RABIH ALAMEDDINE

"HERE DO I DISCOVER
THE HUMILITY
THE MIRACLE OF SUFFERING
WITHOUT SURRENDER
THE MIRACLE OF SUFFERING
WITHOUT DEFEAT"

-JUNE JORDAN

ESCAPE ARTISTS

I left one world & then I came into another. I was premature, so they boxed me in [for safety measures]. I was much bigger than expected, especially for someone born so early. When I asked my mother how long I was incubated, she said, I don't know—I'm not good with time. My first, most intimate contact was with a box. Later, I would become obsessed with magicians.

Let me tell you more about where I come from. Another box told me. The screen glowed & lit up my father's face. He said, everything is burning, everyone is dying, everything is being lost & then...this is where you come from. We sat together while he smoked cigarettes. He gave me a history lesson...He began, "Beirut used to be..." he never finished. "My children are so American," he said to the bedroom, while I was in the bedroom.

I come from a long line of escape artists.

When I was a little girl, I really liked David Copperfield because he got out of a box all chained up, while dunked inside a giant tank. I thought he looked pretty when he wore make-up. I thought he was cool & tough because of how long he held his breath underwater. I used to time myself, to see how long I could hold mine. Many swimming pools kept count. I remember when I broke one minute, one & a half, then—for one hundred & eighty seconds I was invincible.

My father called me his little fish. I said, "No, I'm not a fish, I'm a dolphin." To prove my point, I spat water out of my mouth. I put my hands together & made flippers & splashed & cried out that noise dolphins make when they are playing, when they are trying to communicate with someone they love.

UNDER THE KNIFE

In the fall, at the start of a new semester, you brushed
by me, designer skinny jeans, body waxed bleached

linoleum floors, no more traces of stubborn sideburns.
You wore a tiny new nose. We used to joke about

how we could be sisters. We sat in hallways, cross-
legged, against the cool of lockers. I did not hear

how metal spoke to a distant cousin, sterilized—
I did not know of your alchemy of ruin.

Those storage units of secrets, keepers of classes,
folded notes & magazine cutouts whispered

insults. You pinched excess skin & sighed at
your profile, said: I don't want this mountain on my face.

During break, your family paid a gloved man to hammer,
to slice, & bloody "Little Ararat." He flattened a jutting

peak to acceptable. When you returned, reconstructed,
smelling of burnt hair & perfume, I had to look twice.

You reminded me of home. How could I erase you?

You spent the rest of high school ignoring me
& I forgave you. I was old enough to understand this:

To stop, to look into my eyes, meant to risk reflection.

THE PARTING

I raise my hand to ask my teacher:
          How can one man be everything?
The rest of the class sucks

air through their teeth
          "Do not question God," the teacher says
"But I am asking you, not God!"

"Don't get smart with me!"
          I drift off during all of her classes
& doodle winter   Jump onto the page

skydive freefall a snowflake
          I land in the manger
become a talking lamb

three wise hands stroke my fur
          & I feel a passage of knowledge
enter my coat   sift through me a blessed comb

I search the sky for the North Star
          for all that brings us together
I ask his parents: Are you sad for what is coming?

Each night I get on my knees
          & pray to Jesus   He lives in a frame
above my bed surrounded by silver

His dark sorrowful eyes make
          me feel safe You see me don't you? I say
The curtains move which means yes

I tell him I love him
      I tell him I feel a sea
parting inside of me

I ask him to forgive me
      for any sins that made this sea
I tell him the rip

tide hurts even more
      than when the mean
boy twists my arm

BEIRUT ACHILLES

his new leather shoes broke open the back of his heel
blood began to seep
he climbed with crowded procession
sun branded face with a mark not of his choosing

blood began to seep
can leather shoes exact revenge for having lost their body?
sun branded eyes with a sight not of his choosing
he burned and

can leather shoes exact revenge for remembering their body?
he struggled to ascend to reach the church
he burned and
he continued

he struggled to ascend to reach the church
smelled frankincense before the doors
he continued
how can one evening memorialize a mother?

he dreamed he married myrrh before the doors
keep going no time for mickey mouse games his father said
how can one evening memorialize a mother?
grief imploded at the risk of seeming weak

keep going   no time for mickey mouse games
how to continue?
new leather shoes broke open the back of his heel
grief imploded at the risk of seeming weak

***

new leather shoes broke open the back
of his heel   bloodied dress socks

crowded processions ignored limpers
damp faces sun slapped
& the damned
stain of socks

can leather shoes exact revenge for having lost their body?

continue

sun slapped faces & damp name brand clothes
burned walkers smoke cigarettes

can leather shoes exact revenge for remembering their body?

continue

always ascend must reach church
burned walkers light up slow killers

continue

before the doors nostrils
flared frankincense

continue

how can one evening memorialize a mother?

before the doors he dreamed

he married myrrh

continue
keep going no time for mickey mouse games his father said

                              mother?

father   no games keep time going

how to continue?

WHEN YOU DIED ON ASH WEDNESDAY,

the priest tilted my head to the heavens. The priest painted my forehead with a cross. He said, we return to our origins when we die. For years, I could not wipe the ashes from my face. Grandmother, it's me. You used to call me simply "the girl." Now, I am your grandson. I'm not trapped inside the nets of worlds anymore. Nor do I flap on the decks of boats gasping as my wheeling pupils make their final turn. I swim towards a greater tide. I move between energies like a salmon traveling between rivers & seas. Grandmother, I will tell you what you already know: I have tasted crisp clear water. I have tasted salt.

THE POCKET

"A poem is a small (or large) machine made of words."

- William Carlos Williams

S/he opens the shutters. S/he must check on the runway. S/he must make sure the city is still in order. Airport lights gleam through the humidity like the slicked teeth of a shelter dog. All of them wait for the war to start again. Many say s/he is lucky, s/he gets to go back to America in a few weeks. The landing strip awaits its destiny. Two planes: one departing, one leaving, growl & nearly collide. S/he stands facing the edge of fire, knowing that s/he exists in a pocket of space between two machines: somewhere between home & exile.

CLICK

Ashes ashes I held hands with little girls and we became centrifuges spinning in
dizziness rings who will you marry? Me? I will marry books We all fall down
do you know what it's like when limbs leave your body? When legs break
free from torsos feet blow off from ankles she turned the ignition
a little click and then ... Ashes ashes did her body feel
the loss? I saw her on the news with tubes coming
out from every remaining part of her she didn't
appear to blink this is how we were
introduced did her hand wave
goodbye as it flew away?
Was it like a lover
leaving?

We

      all

          fall

                    down

THE RED PEARL

Teyta had a grocery bag of pennies
on the windowsill, precariously close
to the spitting and hissing radiator.
It made itself known as if it read
my secrets ... I didn't dare dip into
the plastic mouth of the bag, to steal
a little change
to buy sweets,
fearing the bag's snapping jaws
and the radiator's knowledge.

**

I ran around the flat playing,
my tongue flicked a loose tooth,
over and over, until it surrendered,
warm blood filled my mouth.
I burst into Teyta's room proudly
displaying a gummy red pearl.
"I hope the fairy will come!" I said.
Her face remained grave.

That night, I tried to stay awake,
watching shadows made by
the moon, perking up at every sound.
Waiting for flutter, a soft landing,
a brush on my cheek, a whisper.
Fairies only come when
you are asleep, I thought, like mystery.

I stirred when the sun woke me,
my heart beat faster to crinkle
under my pillow.

I pulled out Teyta's grocery bag.
It was heavier than I remembered.
I drew the covers over me,
blocking out the dawning.
All this time *it was her*.

I didn't want money
or sweets anymore.
I wanted the big lie back.

SHHH

You cling to me in the night and the night
is a cloth binding us together ... Every day
I have woken up only for the *possibility* of
tomorrow ...

I've become as small as the thread inside
the cloth binding us together ... You say
even the smallest of things hold power.

You say the windows rattle ... nothing
but thunder ... the smoke ... only the clouds
lowering themselves to sleep ... *shhh, shhh,
shhh* ...

Your arms are hard and smooth around me
I touch your arms in the dark and remember
the wooden slats of my crib ... *shhh, shhh,
shhh* ...

FLESH OF MY FLESH

I walk with a giant of a man.
The giant grabs my hand
squeezes four times
to communicate four words:
do-you-love-me?
& I squeeze back
yes-I-do

Twenty years later, you still
ghost my daily rituals, howl my routine
stop by unexpectedly
sit at the breakfast table reading the newspaper
comfortable in your robe & slippers
you drink slow sips of my coffee
you behave as though you have always lived here

I leave my own house
I walk around the lake
You goose bump my skin
father, I feel you take my hand
but I keep moving
keep the steady pace of appearances

We say nothing because silence
our creation story
& codes all we have known

father, the worst of the growing pains
come from being born from absence
from taking my own rib
& putting my own rib back

to breathe life into my own lungs
to make myself whole
to do this without you

So I sometimes tell myself lies:
I don't miss a stranger
I don't miss my blood

but you, ghost giver of my flesh
you always find a way to return

Sometimes when I walk, I feel you father
you grab my hand & squeeze four times
& despite it all   I always respond

always answer back

Yes-I-do

COIN

If money has no place in houses of worship,
then why does my mouth taste of copper?

SHOOTING S(T)AR

You slip off my plastic coat & hat.
Fill my hard belly insides. Dose me
a perfect line. Wipe off the week &
mark the spot. Save me a place on
your skin. Call me vicious before my
steel sticks you. Brother, I was born
to transform you into an archer.
I crave the sound of go. Pull. Pull.
Release. I am your hot flash spinal
arrow ⇢ my quiver guides flight,
punctures muscle wall. I exodus
old body. You exodus old body. We
blood tangle. I race against your
pulse. Kiss your cells till you sweat
constellations

THE VAULT

i can't visit. my stubble offends you. the curve of my breasts,
not subdued. too many contra-

dictions. the crack in the treble of my throat too deep,
now. we shout over the ocean, gesturing

the same way, talking with our hands. because we share
blood. five years ago, you said protection was

important. you loaded your gun, i reached for your arms.
this is how it has always been between us.

you gave me the key & told me to wait. i unlocked the door
to your room & shivered beside the air

conditioning. on the bedside table was a framed picture—
me on my first day of kindergarten.

my braids were loose & i flashed a crooked smile.
i remember being happy. i got to rock

my favorite outfit: a multi-colored wool vest & a long sleeve shirt.
that clashed. Leaning against the wall

surrounding my image were seven rifles
& AK 47s, to guard your memory of my girlhood.

you can never have too many guns, you said, as
i pulled away from my child self.
if one doesn't work, you can grab another.

there are no pictures of me in the living room.
it's as if your life depends on it.

CALLING SLEEP

Sometimes holding her heart
she feels a deep contraction
as if her blood is struggling to carry
its message to her
she thinks she is too young for this

At night, when the stars create maps
she worries her dreams will swallow her

When calling sleep, she sings

"If the wind could carry me home, where would it take me?"

HUNGER

After the first time,
I nearly took my life, I exhaled
a foreboding wind
into the hellish flames of puberty.

(Though I did not see a man
with a forked tongue.)

All I heard were English bruises
& the rapping of knuckles.

I began to forget
every other language I'd touched.

A cow cried for its mother's milk
out in the pasture.

The horses were restless, shooing flies
as they waited to be brushed.

The myna birds flocked the rooftop.

I do not remember if it was raining
or the color of the sky.

I just collapsed onto the wood floors
and begged the big voice for redemption.

The skinny feral cats meowed outside,
foraging in the garbage to stay alive.

Their hunger surrounded me.

After the first time, I blew a kiss
to them, those wild bones

scavenging

TRAVEL WITHOUT MOVING

All streams flow into the sea, yet the sea is never full.
To the place the streams come from, there they return again.
- Ecclesiastes 1:7

Sometimes I believe I was the one who found you. When the security guard unlocked your door, led him inside, you appeared asleep. Your hands neatly folded under your head, your Bible at your feet. Just resting. I was not your father. You were not my daughter. Yet, how many times did I imagine entering your room, to find you resting this way? How many times did you wake to greet me? Memory recreates memory. I was not there. Yet I returned back to that moment thousands of times. I did not touch you, and flinch at the chill of your skin. I did not collapse onto the floor at the sight of your body, asleep, but not asleep. Still, I believe memory makes us travel without moving. Just as your prayers lifted you from clusters of relentless migraines, protected your eyes from the light, until the end—memory serves to shatter us, or redeem us.

In this case, I tell myself if I was there, perhaps I could have prevented your heart from stopping. We would have stayed up too late watching a detective show, eating popcorn. The arc of the story and the seamless resolution could have comforted us. We'd have risen hung over from too much television and drama, but alive. I can hear the Gospel songs widening the whole apartment, your voice cracking, too carried away to care. I'm not stunned, as your frail frame levitates over breakfast, to the choirs of resurrection. Again, I'm travelling without moving. Everything is so quiet, until the mourning river rushes, to swallow me.

CONTUSION

It was easier for you to imagine yourself
as a priest pressing your palm
on the foreheads of all the men
who attacked you, uttering
you are forgiven & go in peace—
For years, I watched you do the motions
with your hand, as you splashed holy
water. How you bent towards the shade
afraid the sun would cause the cancer
to circle back, covering your arms,
freckles & vestiges of bruises.
You were stronger than any cloaked man.
Who or what was your star of Bethlehem?
How did you survive? I rarely step foot
inside of churches, but I do marvel
at how even the dust is wondrous
when the light comes in. I know
you'd want me there every Sunday
in my best dress, but it's too hard for me
to surrender in a house
that never homed us. That blamed us.
Which world do you live in now? Between realms,
or ascended? Is there nothingness? Is it quiet—
or so full of sound you cover your shadow ears?
Has the pain ceased?
Would you say you are finally free?
Is there chocolate?

INVISIBLE MAN

My forehead touches the ground...
I whisper the words: Subhana Rabil Allah

I thank the gentle prayer rug beneath me
I thank the earth beneath my supplication

In the middle of the room, I appear
as just another Arab man.

The worshippers do not know
that I ask God to give me the strength

to move in this world

as both
a sister and a brother.

THE MAGICIAN'S HANDKERCHIEF

I am the show inciting
laughter & applause,
the magician pulls me
from a black hat by
my floppy ears.
He saws me in half,
rearranges my body
& slides me back together.
I am the serrated grooves
of blade. My sorrow, his red
handkerchief, an endless tugging.
I survive thanks to the wand's gift
of vanishing. I am the dove's release,
the queen of hearts,
the king of spades digging,
the padlock securing my chains,
a belief's need to be bound.

I am the space between levitation

                                                                hovering.

I WILL PLANT MY HANDS IN THE GARDEN
I WILL GROW I KNOW I KNOW I KNOW
AND SWALLOWS WILL LAY EGGS
IN THE HOLLOW OF MY INK-STAINED HANDS

-FOROUGH FARROKHZAD

37

(Tanka)

we shed our husks, age
snake out our past, grow crows feet,
my spider veins,
from grandfather—eyes—both parents
smile? from some ghost in my blood

SYNAPSES

In sickness & awe
I fall to my knees

I propose my affections
to my ailing chromosome

I build a boat out of plastic
prescription bottles

weave a sail binding
sinews and lesions

any honey moon we take
means crossing over bones

there are no stars where we travel
only electric synapses striking tissue sky

only the rivers of blood from our hearts
to our brains

Answer our despair

FUNCTIONAL SOMATIC SYNDROME

You live every part of me
in the crumble of my womb's drying flower

In the dance of my cells separation

Your majesty hides within
my cramping forest of muscle

If we are in this for life
Speak.

Tongue me into mystery

Take me inside
your Goddess

I will enter
the
narrow
space
of
my
own
cave.

I will wait to receive you

MIGRATORY GLOSSITIS

(for Ibrahim Baba)

i have been asked for my papers, more than once, to prove
ancestry. but i was denied, i only have word of stories & traces
of relations—letters. my entry into adulthood spawned a rejection
of indigenousness. it had to do with not feeling "enough"
but that is another story, longer than this poem.

Joseph, my friend, who i loved, when i said,
we don't come from the same tribe
but we share something unspoken, he was silent—
named after the father of Christ, who was not a white man,
but painted so, a picket fence revision, he too carried
a mixed complex. my mother & grandfather, told too pale
to be Indian, yet still claiming, till the end.
handing that claim to me. enough.

***

i woke one morning to another new symptom, my tongue
blazed with territories. diagnosed as geographic tongue
or mapped tongue, a condition where my tongue formed
ridges, its borders appeared & disappeared, a living history.
second by second it morphed into new countries, lines
displaced & recreated. they dissolved into my spit before
being reborn. i remember the doctor, how she shined
her light inside my mouth & said, "you mean to tell me,
your tongue is always changing, it never stays the same?"
and she gazed upon me as if realizing for the first time
that nothing is truly stagnant.

to her, my teeth rose like unearthed temples
& all of this between the clenching of my jaw.
it's a mystery. the underground root canal
of suffering, how there seems to be not one cure

to the crisis of identity. when the tears trailed down
i tasted the saline of my wounding, a forced passage
that i (re) named the ocean, to ease the burden of
being called extinct, while still remaining here.

THE EDGE OF YOUR PAPER

If my symptoms are just in my head, then why can't you look me in the eye? Why do you gaze past me, like so many do, seeing projections of smoke & deserts, men, with more beard than me, some darker, some lighter, but always ready to blow kisses. I'm here, sitting on the edge of your paper, with stained photographs of sandy shores. I'm telling you about how I can't go on like this anymore. You scribble something down. You talk to me about vacationing in Israel one summer. I've been sick, I say. Exhausted. It's hard to breathe. I'm losing my memory. I'm too young to not remember. Have I told you this before? How I'm here, sitting on the edge of your paper, with stained photographs of sandy shores. I see parachutes coming down when I'm trying to sleep. I smell the leather of military grade boots. I hear the cry of the skin that once was. No, I can't count sheep, only metal underbellies. I can't go on this way anymore. You scribble something down. You talk to me about vacationing in Israel one summer. Have I said this already? I'm losing my memory. I'm too young to not remember. Are you afraid of my beauty? Are you afraid of explosive blossoms, the color of your tears? Am I repeating myself? Are you afraid of my name, the way you can't pronounce it properly? Are you comfortable being able to enunciate my illnesses perfectly? Are you pleased with the school that taught you acronyms dull pain? My mouth is so dry. Doctor, do you think I've been drinking too much ink from the daily news? Have I told you this before? How I fear losing my own humanity? Have I told you that watered down language washes faces away? Have we spoken of how dilution makes it easier to kill?

7 SEAS

I'm going to listen to your heart, the doctors say.
As if, an instrument can capture
a heart... They shine
their lights in my eyes,
my nostrils flare, filled
with alcohol & cold metal notes

It's their job to sometimes forget   my body houses a person,

my skin   my earth, 7 seas within me.

I want to remind them we are all approximately 60% water,

but the examination room stifles my voice.

Cough, the doctors say, listening to my lungs.

On a scale of 1-10...how much pain are you in today?

I cannot quantify pain, nor answer them honestly, when words debilitating
              linger in my throat, so

I hang on

to the purr of my cat curled beside me,
to red wildflowers outside,
to the hummingbird fiending for nectar,
to the laughter of children,
to a poem I've read before,

that still shivers like it's the first time.

PRAYERS FOR MY 17TH CHROMOSOME

Where did my illness begin?

Did it begin before
in another realm
in a galaxy of cells?

stars of nuclei?

Did it begin in the womb?
when I was submerged inside the sea of my mother

who was submerged
in the sea of God,

liquor, whitewash, cigarette
smoke & the aching tendons of war—were

generations of violence
those strands of DNA, the roots
of my rioting

17th chromosome,
  am I sick because of all of this?

or was it just that when I was in the womb
forming further into being,
my body was overcome with joy
with spontaneity,

like a classical symphony   abandoning   the scripts,

to play the sounds of each
of their creation stories

Again, was it God?
who some believe
is 1
who some say made Earth
in 7 days,

is this the Divine
within
manifesting
as 1 and 7 linked
to become
17

and if 1 plus 7 equals 8
then am I 8?

Who will consume my rapid cells
multiplying into tumors?

How do I accept an illness incurable

life-long?

Today, I'm too exhausted to debate religion, mathematics & science.
I decide to invite my 17th chromosome over for dinner.
We've been living in the same house,
but eating separately.

Hmm... I wonder how many extra plates will I need?
Plates or platelets? my 17th chromosome says.

Well, at least my disease has a sense of humor.

And so, my heart murmurs,
let us begin by simplifying:

by making room,

for all of us to talk
for all of us to listen
for all of us to enjoy this meal
together.

doctors make forceps with their fingers. they imitate the smallest violin. your pain is not a note but a whine. you have come to know how they cope when confronted with the unknown. the oxycodone numbs 1/4 of your thumb, but leaves you swimming in your bath. splashing, convinced you are a rubber ducky. you laugh when you are alone. your voice is a stranger and a friend.

YOUR BODY BURNS IN YOUR ROOM

you salute the landscape from the square acre of bed

as for the peeled wallpaper: it's a rolling wave,

a leaf curling, anything, but the fetal position,

it's a bastion of ribbons in your hair,

it's a smoke signal formed from a sciatic spark

rising to your ceiling, forming itself into

a genderless God. It's the miracle you can't undo,

the waking up even when you don't want to,

how you create from rock bottom, the dirt under

your nails, the half moons, the scars in the night sky

OUT OF THE SOIL

you pushed
little root—dark & wet

you were a freckle under a tango of weeds
until you surged, rose
& we applauded

GRAND DESIGN
(for M81 and the rest of us)

today collect the dazzling shelter of flowers
stitch a crown large enough for the globe
fragrant enough for satellites to lift their noses
take the prayer of night into your arms
as she sleeps, breathe with her
breathe with the night
there are times when there is nothing
left to do, but create
form the unseen into a tangible communion
of stardust, place the galaxy on your tongue
let your mouth be a wondrous glow
your words a beacon
when everything is lost
imagine yourself as more than an earth-
quaking body a gift
the streaking tail of a comet
become that which holds your eye
that which makes you gasp

WHEN I COME BACK, I COME BACK AS WIND

I.

Do you hear me? wind whistling in the dark
moving through your house speaking to you
slapping rain on your windows

that breeze caressing your face
lifting your hair
just yesterday, when you stepped outside

I turned foxtails into rattles
so you could be reminded of me

I banded together a symphony
of grass & leaves when you leaned against
the bough of the cypress tree

II.

I am no longer hunted
It's impossible to capture or detain me
I pass through the grates of every Guantanamo
& kiss the bearded & smooth cheeked missing
carry the rain to each thirsty open mouthed refugee plea

III.

Let me be clear, I do not participate in the mosh
pit of tsunamis or hurricanes or typhoons
why would I return formless only to be consumed by rage?

I am pure element
with fire, water & earth beside me

sky colors embrace me but I feel no more blues

as raw a sensation as visceral   the way a drummer lets loose
when she has her solo all thump & snare

sky colors embrace me but I feel no more blues

              & high hat

riffing off heart beats & gourds & buckets

sky colors embrace me but I feel no more blues

every surface a possible beat   music
even without a body

I know how to fill a room

sky colors embrace me but I feel no more blues

I am there against your fingers underneath
frets & worries

I travel freely
in the belly of guitars playing love songs
sky colors embrace me how I feel no more blues

55

OUR DANGEROUS SWEETNESS

When I hear the news
another one of us has been killed
my heart constricts
I reach with a frantic grief
towards a soothing balm, difficult to find

And I can't help but think of
all the times my own life has been threatened
of all the people I love
and their own lives

I am tired of being afraid
to speak my name
to unbind my chest
to be feminine and masculine

to go outside

I am tired of being afraid
of being brown

I am tired of being afraid
of my own existence
of revealing my full self
for fear that if I do, I will be killed

Here: I am the living impossibility
like so many of the people I love
who have the audacity to embrace themselves

Each day
I feel departed souls swirl surround me
I feel thousands of hands brushing away my tears

They say: do what you were born to do

To write these words down
To write myself into wholeness
To write myself away from vengeance

They say: listen and so I listen
For a long time, I listen

And then they say speak
to those that are still here
& so I speak
to those of you still here

I speak to say:
My Dear Beautiful People,
Each time you are broken,
I break, I break,   I break a little more
then un-break

I am piecing myself back together
with the care of a potter's hands
I clay phoenix

I feel the heat
of our resurrections burning
to glaze our skin into glow
my fire and my kiln

are these words, this space
the intimate threads
of our connection

my prayer: we remember
ourselves as entwined in this struggle
my prayer: we undo the knots we have tied around ourselves
we breathe
we remember we can be bound together
& free

I write because I feel the pulse of us
chanting the names of those who have died

Our own names
Our essences as holy

I envision us going on
to eclipse, building, bigger, bigger, bigger
more luminous

So bright

My beautiful people
our breaking is our making
& if I strip all my other identities away:

I am simply a poet who listens
To God
To the dead
To the living
To all left behind
To all the places in between

I am simply a poet
who writes these words because I believe in us
because I know a faith uncontainable by an alphabet

My beautiful people let us dream towards
what we want
beyond survival

Let us dream towards loving ourselves
till we become love over and over again

My beautiful people
I can taste our honeyed victory

My beautiful people
our dangerous sweetness
is our rebellion

NEY

take apart the hollow bone
drill holes
carve & smooth
this former lover of flesh
construct our flute
let us blow our breath
play the harmony of our grandmothers'
resurrections over Aleppo
while all the sunken
tombstones cry out: we want to return

every morning   we dress ourselves
in another country
and there is nobody to shout
when the bombs fall
just a loud whistle & a terrible
silence   we stir in our beds

we wake covered in sweat
the millions of refugees
pills we can't swallow
they remain
lodged inside our throats

we drink too much coffee
to function
haunted by guns
we don't even pack
it doesn't matter
how many birdhouses we build
someone will always say
we're vigilantes

we watch Aleppo in grainy footage
we wave to our cousins
over the airwaves
and hope satellites
can deliver embraces

in the diaspora we sink
into chairs   we open a book to escape
while the libraries in our homelands
are set ablaze   our stories prayers
and histories burn into smoke filled
tornadoes schools explode with children
still at their desks

churches mosques and temples
now rubble   news crews
film carnage and wailing
zooming in on our anger
calling us criminals
never our names no never our names
only collateral collateral collateral

here in the diaspora
I can't even mourn in Arabic
I've forgotten the language
but at night   I still dream with my people
I dream that I am crossing borders with my cousins
under a quiet sky
and we take turns carrying one another

at night when I dream
I sing all of our true names

CACTUS FLOWER

'We flash victory signs in the darkness, so the darkness may glitter.'
- Mahmoud Darwish

As the sun sets—we set our plan into motion.
Our sole purpose to overthrow

any assumptions, to change
the course of ordinary thinking.

Our work begins by speaking to darkness
and telling darkness   soon :

      we will demonstrate through the secrecy of stars,

earth's magnetic embrace
how we can be many things at once.

So much of the work we do
is internal, goes unnoticed, uncompensated.

We get written off or not written at all,
labeled freakish, prickled,
rough around the edges.

We learn to thrive
in the dry humor of soil;
carry water in our bellies
to quench our own thirst.

We survive, over again.
Adapt. Even after being
carried in the beaks of birds,
dropped elsewhere,
far from our roots, we grow.

We flourish.
And when least expected, when histories
not told by us, for us, claim we are defeated,

we gather our tears as dew.   We release our anguish,
intoxicated by our own sexed pollen.

We burst,

displaying the luscious folds of our petals.

RISK

We bridge broken wood,
repair the rotten slats that creak.

We restore the lifeless vine,
braid vitality from decay.

The way of crossing is never easy,
someone always looks down. We tremble

knowing how far we can fall. We question
who or what will cushion us. We feel our frailty.

We love, as tremors rock earth,
bound in devastation & slow transition.

We love, the way erosion
paints complex striations.

Vulnerable, the way exposed mountains
remember being covered by the ocean.

How we love, through each disaster,
Praise us, how much we risk
with every reach.

INTO SOON THE SKY

I.

she grows wings to fly
over the wall
built through her country

wings   hues of sunsets
i ebb with her
my bones lurch

when feathers break

my skin,   i dream
of cement each night, the dust

of rebuilding

she soars into the sky   so
we can meet in the clouds

and kiss our way back to our childhoods

we turn an olive tree
into a straw
to drink up the dead sea

she tells me it's possible to have a tower
inside of yourself
a militia inside your marrow

we dress our own wounds
before we undress each other

I grows wings

to fly over
the wall

my body, one
piece of strong

& delicate science intuiting pilot
muscle   memory
migration on   re-
collection

i watch her gain
momentum
I watch her soar
I'm not afraid of her abandoning me
I know she needs to go higher
before she can come down again

II.

we flap our arms
until they blur
from dawn into the dusky
hues of sunsets

our
weight
becoming
weightless

she sees me watching her
sends a birdsong down my throat
I sing her song back to her
so she knows I have not forgotten her

for so many nights   we have dreamt of cement
so many nights
we have dreamt of one another's face
smelled the dank odor
of rebuilding
after fires   after missiles

cruising

we have inhaled the sorrow that comes with piles of

missing

for many years, it has been difficult to think of
butterflies

when caterpillars tear through houses
as easy as
leaves

III.

maybe this is how we learned to feed ourselves
though we still chirp to each other
please wake me gently
in the morning

we have had to grow wings
she said not to escape
but to become ourselves

at noon we meet in the clouds
she takes a branch & turns it into a straw
we drink from the dead sea
to replenish our tears which have gone dry

I tell her I have a tower inside of myself
a militia inside my marrow
she says the army of men inside my chest
are only now starting to leave

we dress our wounds
we undress each other
to rest in the nest we have made

later she tells me to not be afraid
to fly higher
let your inner compass lead you she says

so intuition becomes my pilot
our muscle memory synchronized
we migrate
gain momentum

we fly to cyprus for the evening
our wings blurring into arms
and back to wings until we meld
into the dusky hues of sunsets

when I grow tired she reminds me to sing
I send a birdsong to her throat
and she sings back to me
so I know I will not be forgotten
I do not miss the certainty of
only having arms

IV.

we have dreamt of cement
so many nights

of infrastructure hurtling from the dirt

we have dreamt of each other's faces

we have smelled the dank odor
of re building
after fires after missiles   cruising

inhaled the sorrow that comes with piles of

missing

we try to find beauty all around us
but it has been difficult to appreciate butterflies
when caterpillars tear through houses
as easy as leaves

before we sleep, we chirp to one another
please wake me gently in the morning

at noon   we meet in the clouds
I take a branch and turn it into a straw
we drink from the dead sea
to replenish our tears which have gone dry

we dress our wounds
before undressing each other

inside the nest we press
feather to feather

breast to breast
she tells me she has a tower inside of herself
a militia inside her marrow

I say the army of men inside my chest
are only now starting to leave

DAWNING / A STONE

After Amina Said

I come from the shores
of grace & ash.
I am not so different that I do not also fight against emptiness.
I fill my time to escape the demands
of a body that does the opposite
of what I want. Have you ever considered why we are so uneasy?
Or that all human beings were once the size of a small stone,
no larger than an eye, curled inside of darkness?
Whoever says only light
means good, draws borders & creates erasure.
History proves this, We are the dust
& the clay, the timeless & the finite.
We can spend our whole lives aimless, but we all return
to the grave.
A child asked me, do we become winged?
I said, I don't know. I just want to live as a gift.
I don't find passion
in exile,
or dread,
or instant gratification. I find it in the bliss
of a poem,
& the possibility of creating a new here, in the shadow
of a branch,
in the transcendence
of tongue.
My wish is that where we go next, we will span a song
larger than the sun.
We will forget solitude.
We will revolt against fate
& bare our faces
We will become the endless,
the source,
the horizon
awakening

NOTES

The poem "Prayers for My 17th Chromosome" is based on the experience of the author living with the genetic condition, Neurofibromatosis Type 1, which is a cell mutation of the 17th chromosome.

"When I Come Back, I Come Back As Wind," was inspired by the following quote:

> "Y'know, Music is a beautiful thing. When I'm reincarnated, I'm gonna come back as a musical note! That way can't nobody capture me. They can use the hell out of me but ain't nothin' too much they can do to me. They can mess me up. They can play the wrong note. They can play a C, but they can't really destroy a C. All it is, is a tone. So I'm gonna come back as a note!" — Rahsaan Roland Kirk

"Dawning / A Stone" is a golden shovel, a poetic form invented by Terrance Hayes.

"Into Soon the Sky" is a line pulled from the song "Bird Gurhl" by Antony and the Johnsons.

ACKNOWLEDGMENTS

Thank you to the editors of the following journals and anthologies, in which these poems—some in different versions—originally appeared:

backroomlive blog: "Beirut Achilles," and "The Parting"

Bird's Thumb: "Grand Design"

Collective Brightness: LGBTIQ Poets on Faith, Religion and Spirituality, edited by Kevin Simmonds: "Invisible Man"

Cream City Review: "Migratory Glossitis"

The Feminist Wire: "Risk, and Your Body Burns in Your Room"

Foglifter: "Ney," and "Dawning/A Stone"

580 Split: "Under the Knife"

Flicker and Spark: A Contemporary Queer Anthology of Spoken Word and Poetry, edited by Regie Cabico and Brittany Fonte: "Flesh of My Flesh"

Gender Outlaws: The Next Generation, edited by Kate Bornstein and S. Bear Bergman: "shooting s(T)ar"

Kweli: "The Pocket"

Nimrod: "The Magician's Handkerchief "

Sukoon: "The Edge of Your Paper"

13 After: "Shh," and "Click"

Troubling the Line: Trans and Genderqueer Poetry and Poetics, edited by TC Tolbert and Trace Peterson: "Escape Artists," "Cactus Flower," "Prayers for My 17th Chromosome," and "When You Died on Ash Wednesday"

Writing the Walls Down: A Convergence of LGBTQ Voices, edited by Helen Klonaris and Amir Rabiyah: "Your Body Burns in Your Room," and "Our Dangerous Sweetness"

GRATITUDE

Thank you to the Creator, Mother Mary, and all of my other spiritual guides, including Ibrahim Baba and my Sufi community. Without your prayers, love, and guidance, I would not have been able to complete this book.

Thank you to the friends, teachers, and writers who had faith in my work before I did, and/or who have supported me over the years: Helen Klonaris, Elmaz Abinader, Suheir Hammad, Celeste Chan, Daphne Gottlieb, Tiffany Higgins, Ahimsa Timoteo Bodhrán, Randa Jarrar, Tomi Knutson, Janine Mogannam, Krys Méndez Ramirez, Trish Salah, A.j. Alana Ka'imi Bryce, Mari Esabel Valverde, Talya, Andrea Assaf, Nico Dacumos, Angele Ellis, Kin Folkz, Nia King, Shawna Sodersten, Manzel Bowman, Seth Pennington, RAWI (The Radius of Arab-American Writers), Marilyn Nelson, Trace Peterson, TC Tolbert, Kimmel Harding Nelson Center for the Arts, Sean Dorsey, Shawna Virago, June Jordan's Poetry for the People at UC Berkeley, Aya de Leon, and the Voices of Our Nations (VONA) crew. Thank you to Rajiv Mohabir and Naomi Shihab Nye for your brilliant blurbs. Your poetry has deeply transformed me.

Thank you to Bryan Borland for believing in this book!

Also, I humbly ask that you please forgive me if I left any names off that should be here. Please know it does not come from ill intent, rather human error.

ABOUT THE POET

Amir Rabiyah is a two-spirit disabled queer femme poet and writing coach. They were born in London to a Cherokee and European mother and a Syrian and Lebanese father. Their work explores living life on the margins and at the intersections of multiple identities. Amir writes about living with chronic pain and illness, war, trauma, spirituality, and redemption, and speaks on silenced places. Amir is the co-editor of *Writing the Walls Down: A Convergence of LGBTQ Voices*, and has published in numerous anthologies and journals. They believe domestic work, chanting Sufi prayers over a home-cooked meal, and nurturing our communities is crucial for revolution.

ABOUT THE PRESS

Sibling Rivalry Press is an independent press based in Little Rock, Arkansas. It is a sponsored project of Fractured Atlas, a nonprofit arts service organization. Contributions to support the operations of Sibling Rivalry Press are tax-deductible to the extent permitted by law, and your donations will directly assist in the publication of work that disturbs and enraptures. To contribute to the publication of more books like this one, please visit our website and click *donate*.

Sibling Rivalry Press gratefully acknowledges the following donors, without whom this book would not be possible:

TJ Acena	JP Howard	Tina Parker
Kaveh Akbar	Shane Khosropour	Brody Parrish Craig
John-Michael Albert	Randy Kitchens	Patrick Pink
Kazim Ali	Jørgen Lien	Dennis Rhodes
Seth Eli Barlow	Stein Ove Lien	Paul Romero
Virginia Bell	Sandy Longhorn	Robert Siek
Ellie Black	Ed Madden	Scott Siler
Laure-Anne Bosselaar	Jessica Manack	Alana Smoot Samuelson
Dustin Brookshire	Sam & Mark Manivong	Loria Taylor
Alessandro Brusa	Thomas March	Hugh Tipping
Jessie Carty	Telly McGaha & Justin Brown	Alex J. Tunney
Philip F. Clark	Donnelle McGee	Ray Warman & Dan Kiser
Morell E. Mullins	David Meischen	Ben Westlie
Jonathan Forrest	Ron Mohring	Valerie Wetlaufer
Hal Gonzlaes	Laura Mullen	Nicholas Wong
Diane Greene	Eric Nguyen	Anonymous (18)
Brock Guthrie	David A. Nilsen	
Chris Herrmann	Joseph Osmundson	

CPSIA information can be obtained
at www.ICGtesting.com
Printed in the USA
FFHW02n0635300918
48589854-52524FF